CAPTURED IN STONE

CAPTURED IN STONE:

CARVING CANADA'S PAST

R. ELEANOR MILNE

WITH K. BARBARA LAMBERT AND ELEANOR MOORE

MARGARET WADE LABARGE AND EWALD RICHTER

PENUMBRA PRESS

PENUMBRA PRESS

Captured In Stone is a first edition published by Penumbra Press. Edited for the Press by Douglas Campbell. Printed in Canada.

The Igloolik song on page 24 is from Harold Seidelman and James Turner, *Inuit Imagination: Arctic Myth and Sculpture*, Toronto: Douglas & McIntyre Ltd., 1993.

"The Spell of the Yukon" by Robert W. Service on page 72 is used by permission of the Estate of Robert W. Service.

As cited, photographs are from the following sources: National Archives of Canada, Ewald Richter, Laurence Hayward Collection, and the Eleanor Milne Collections.

NATIONAL LIBRARY OF CANADA CATALOGUING IN PUBLICATION

Lambert, K. Barbara, 1923-
    Captured in stone : carving Canada's past / K. Barbara Lambert, R. Eleanor Milne, and Eleanor Moore ; introduction by M.W. Labarge.

Includes bibliographical references.
ISBN 1-894131-32-0

    1. Stone carving—Ontario—Ottawa. 2. Friezes—Ontario—Ottawa. 3. Centre Block (Parliament Buildings, Ottawa, Ont.) 4. Milne, Eleanor. I. Milne, Eleanor II. Moore, Eleanor III. Title.

NA4415.C22O77 2002a   736'.5'0971384   C2002-905895-3

The publisher gratefully acknowledges the Canada Council for the Arts and the Ontario Arts Council for supporting Penumbra Press's publishing programme. The publisher acknowledges the financial support of the Government of Canada through the Book Publishing Industry Development Program (BPIDP) for our publishing activities.

CONTENTS

DEDICATION

This book is dedicated to all who come to visit the Centre Block, Canada's Parliament Buildings.

ACKNOWLEDGEMENTS

The *History of Canada Series* is only one of the many carved works of art that are part of the essential fabric of the Centre Block of Canada's Parliament Buildings. The books that will tell of other works remain to be written.

The Right Honourable Roland Michener, Speaker of the House of Commons and E.A. Gardner, Chief Architect of Public Works, approved the design concept.

During the design process, Erik Spicer, Parliamentary Librarian, gave me unlimited access to the stacks, a priceless source of information and historical reference.

Gerald Williams, Deputy Minister of Public Works, Walter Dicks, Regional Manager, and Henry Carr, Building Manager, supported the sculpture program in many ways.

Over the years, the staff carried out unexpected requests. The Corps of Commissionaires, in their capacity as guardians of the building, gave us the security we needed to work at night.

In 1981, George Wilkes, humanitarian and collector of art, suggested publication of a book on all carvings and stained glass windows in the Centre Block that had been made since 1962. This book is the first to develop that idea.

My heartfelt thanks go out to the Society of the Sacred Heart, without whose financial support I would not have had the courage to embark on the project.

Audrey Dubé, Assistant Parliamentary Curator, House of Commons, whose interest in and knowledge of the history of the Parliament Buildings dates back to the time when she was a valued member of the research staff in the Parliamentary Library, gave liberally of her files.

The vivid and convincing images at the heart of this book were produced by photographer extraordinaire Ewald Richter and his assistant Christine Richter.

The floor plan of the Foyer was finely drawn and lettered by hand by architect Michael T. Lambert.

Through the sensitivity of our publisher, John Flood, Penumbra Press, and the meticulous workmanship of our editor, Douglas Campbell, the waters have been cleared of verbal detritus and awkwardness of expression — they have made it possible for us to speak in our own collective voice.

A special thanks to Margaret Wade Labarge, medieval scholar, wise counsellor, and friend. And thanks also to my two collaborators, K. Barbara Lambert and Eleanor Moore, whose knowledge of the nature of architecture and love of the history and culture of Native Peoples were placed at the service of a deeper understanding of the art of the Centre Block.

— *R. Eleanor Milne*

For many Canadians, their first sight of Parliament Hill, with its view of the Ottawa River and its magnificent ensemble of neo-Gothic Parliament Buildings, is a heart-warming reminder of the riches of their Canadian heritage. Once they enter the Centre Block, which holds the chambers of the House of Commons and the Senate, they discover that while the stone exterior is indeed majestic, the inside of the building is home to an equally remarkable collection of stone carvings. A number of stone carvers have worked on the building over the years, both inside and out. In 1961, however, the Department of Public Works, which is responsible for government buildings, decided it was time to carve sculptures in the actual fabric of the Centre Block that would express historical and symbolic themes relevant to Canada. The first group, which occupies the place of honour in the Foyer of the House of Commons, was created between 1962 and 1974. It tells in stone a wide span of the history of Canada and the people who made that history. Stone carvings, like other works of art, often tell their stories in a way that can be made clearer to the average spectator with a little interpretation. This book hopes to serve as an informed introduction to the wealth of fact and symbol that lies within these stones, so that the visitor can not only enjoy the artistic achievement, but also better understand the important events in our history that these panels portray.

When, in 1961, the government decided to embark on this major project, the Department of Public Works was instructed to search for a sculptor who would be able, both artistically and technically, to flesh out and carve in stone this still unexplored idea. The unexpected result of the competition, which attracted twenty men and one woman, was the choice of Eleanor Milne, the only one who possessed the background and skills that would enable her to elaborate, design, and carry out in stone the government proposal. Fortunately, the appointment recognized the remarkable diversity of skills that were needed and that she could bring to bear in meeting this formidable challenge. Because the successful candidate would be expected to work in a variety of media, the position was renamed Dominion Sculptor, and Eleanor Milne filled it with distinction from 1962 to 1993.

A sketch of Eleanor Milne's background will suggest how her varied talents and skills were developed. Her father was a naval architect and her mother a painter, and their children were encouraged at an early age to draw and sketch. Born in Saint John, New Brunswick, in 1925, Eleanor, like her older sister and younger brother, learned to know and love the Maritimes in her early childhood. In 1936, the family moved to Montreal, where Eleanor learned French and benefited from the ability of an inspired teacher to find the key to the mind of this intelligent and promising, but dyslexic, teenager. Although she may have had trouble with reading, she had none with design. After high school she studied at the Montreal Museum School of Fine Arts, at the time when Arthur Lismer, the Group of Seven painter, was its principal, and also took the opportunity — to Lismer's astonishment — to study anatomy with medical students at McGill University. There she had the extraordinary experience of drawing in the operating room for Dr. Wilder Penfield, the great neurological surgeon. A stint in 1945-1946 at the Central College of Arts and Crafts in London, England enabled her to acquire engraving skills, and her time in Europe also introduced her to the old-world treasures of Romanesque and Gothic architecture, stone carving, and sculpture, which had a considerable influence on her later work. Back in Montreal at l'École des beaux-arts, she continued her studies in wood engraving, but also began to carve in wood, under the tutelage of the well-known wood sculptor, Sylvia Daoust. Finally, at Syracuse University, she worked in a post-graduate course under Ivan Mestrovic. This internationally famous Yugoslav sculptor was best known for his large figures, powerfully designed and boldly cut, but much of his work also had a strong spiritual element, and his enduring influence can often be seen in Eleanor Milne's own varied work. Beginning in the 1950s she not only worked as a sculptor in wood, stone, and bronze, but also painted and experimented with the making of stained glass. This remarkably diverse experience suggests why the selection committee felt that she was the right person to entrust with the job.

As she became familiar with the existing carvings in the Parliament Buildings, Eleanor Milne's first task in creating the frieze of the history of Canada was to discover the specific events and symbols with which she could design an intelligible whole that could be carved in stone within the allotted space. Her necessary research included not only the more usual scholarly resources, but also diaries and private journals. This study reinforced her own sense of the importance of recognizing the contribution of many individuals in the making of Canadian history.

Eleanor Milne is a very modest woman, and she has always insisted that credit be given to the devoted team of able stone carvers with whom she worked. Their contribution was certainly essential, but they in turn recognized that she was not only the supervisor, and the major sculptor of the figures, but also the one with the vision, the intelligence, and the artistic ability to bring the frieze to a successful realization.

Her artistic contribution to the Parliament Buildings was not confined to this set of panels. In 1970, she collaborated with Russell Goodman in the design, fabrication, and installation of the stained glass windows in the Chamber of the House of Commons. When this project is considered along with her own work in the Parliament Buildings and her individual commissions, not only on Parliament Hill but for other legislative buildings, she is revealed as an artist of incredible productivity. In her more than thirty years as Dominion Sculptor, which ended with her retirement in 1993, Eleanor Milne left a valuable legacy to Canada. In the work that adorns the Parliament Buildings she celebrates the land and the people she knows and loves. Her imprint on the precincts of Parliament Hill, especially the Centre Block, is quite literally carved in stone.

— *Margaret Wade Labarge, CM*
Medieval Historian
Adjunct Professor, Carleton University
Ottawa, Canada

Soaring above the green copper peaks and spires of a jagged and picturesque skyline, the Peace Tower has become the generally recognized symbol of Canada. Centrally placed on the front façade of the long stone building that houses Canada's parliament, it seems to pierce the sky. At the tower's foot, the main entrance welcomes all, but forward thrusts of the wall at either end of the long building mark more restricted entries — to the Foyer of the Senate on the east and that of the House of Commons on the west. Only members of parliament are privileged to pass through the broad oak door of the Members' Private Entrance and ascend the twin-branched marble staircase that leads into the Foyer of the House of Commons. This spacious inner courtyard may be entered from several other directions, but the public approaches it from the wide ceremonial corridor that links the House of Commons to the Senate.

The Foyer is an impressive sight. The eye runs up powerful columns and along wide curves of pointed arches with their decorative carvings, is stopped momentarily by a broad band of boldly sculptured frieze that forms the *History of Canada Series*, then continues upward past narrower, more delicate arches to a strip of carving just below the ceiling. After roving over the strong geometrical pattern of the concrete frame enclosing the silvery-grey painted glass ceiling, the eye moves down to catch sight of paintings and individual sculptures on the lower walls, and, over distant doorways, carvings by Aboriginal artists.

There is an immediate sense of invitation, of weightlessness and light, an effect created by the size of the space, the proportion of the arches, and the height of the ceiling, but also by the constant variations in the natural light.

The scene has become familiar to all who watch the television news, because it is here, when the House is in session, that the media scrum is often played out — journalists jostling each other with their tape recorders, politicians squinting in the glare of powerful quartz lights, and now and then glimpses of many artistic works.

The ornamentation of the Foyer is made up of many elements, and many hands have contributed to it. The makers of the *History of Canada Series* frieze carved directly into the limestone at mezzanine level. Five metres (15 feet) above the floor, measuring close to 40 metres (120 feet) long by 1.5 metres (4.5 feet) high, it is divided into ten sets. Each consists of two panels in low relief and a central stone in high relief.

The completed work captures in lyric fashion the story of life in that part of the North American continent now called Canada. The basic theme is punctuated by particular events that mark turning points in the evolution of the nation. Beginning at the east wall and ending at the north wall, the whole is an expression of linear time interwoven with timeless allegorical comments that build to a note of hope.

— *K. Barbara Lambert & Eleanor Moore*

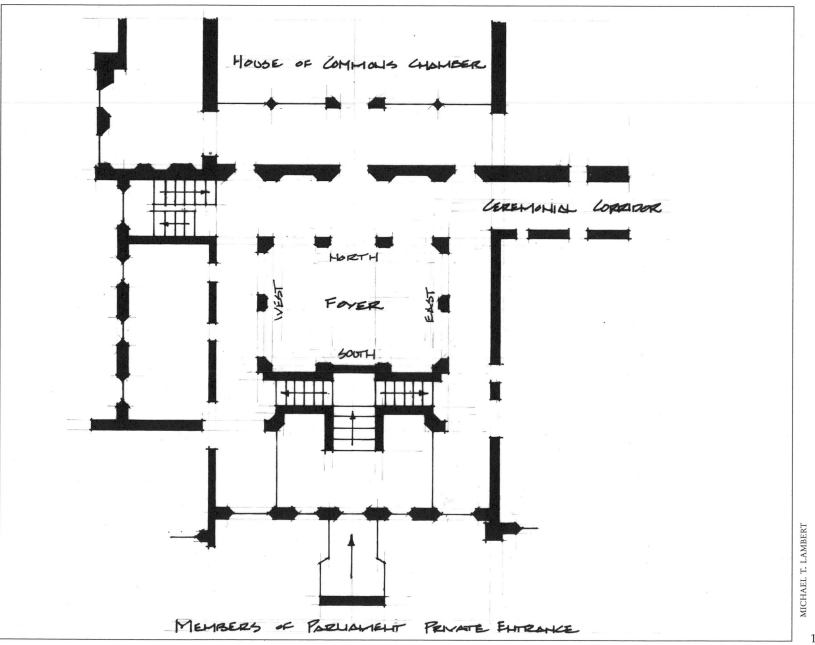

HOUSE OF COMMONS CHAMBER

CEREMONIAL CORRIDOR

NORTH

WEST   FOYER   EAST

SOUTH

MEMBERS OF PARLIAMENT PRIVATE ENTRANCE

EWALD RICHTER

12

The air hoses are already installed when the carving team arrives at work. We carve by hand with mallet and chisel and by air-power using pneumatic hammers, carbide tip chisels and drill. The long scaffolding holds us high above the floor, and allows ample space for each of us to swing our hammers and to cut and chisel. We start at eleven at night, we stop for lunch at two in the morning, and leave for home at six in the early dawn or in the black pre-dawn of winter.

We are on site, cutting directly into the stone of the Foyer of the House of Commons, in the Centre Block on Parliament Hill. This is a handsome building. After the lunch break, I walk alone in the main corridor. A soft glow rises in tones of tan from the marble paving and from the stone walls quarried from a now dry seabed, rife with fossils of the squid family, corals and other ancient life. I am at home here. I cherish the reassuring warmth and the silence, broken only by our tools and voices. In the quiet, the building seems to be breathing. My imagination quickens as I sense the vitality of the milieu awakening my own creativity. As I walk, I come to understand that changing the form of the wild, untamed stone is more a matter of inviting the resisting stuff to accept a new presence than of imposing a new form, a new life, upon it.

We are engaged in making low relief sculpture in a frieze running free along all four walls. Interrupting the continuous flow are high relief stones which stand out from the running document but which must not disrupt the vitality of line and rhythm. I have already designed the master drawings, and now draw them full scale in charcoal onto the stone, in readiness for each of us to do our part in transforming the lineal image into three dimensions. Each cut must be thought out as

Anton Nielsen, Joseph Joanisse, and Eleanor Milne at work.

13

the work progresses and potential errors caught quickly, so that corrections or modifications can be made.

As designer, it is easy to deal with problems that arise, and easy to have discussions on suggestions of a better way to express a turn of leaf or curl of wave, or to explain why changes may not be made.

Working with the carvers is a special pleasure. The work is so absorbing that our lives are almost totally devoted to the job. There are times when the realization of the form is so surprising and so delightful that we lay aside our tools, lower the canvas wall of the scaffolding, climb down and sit in a row on the marble floor, admiring the elegant solution. We take a little time to cool ourselves and rest. In winter, the temperature on the scaffold often reaches almost ninety degrees. Summer is even hotter and very humid. At the end of our night's toil, we are dusted with fine powdered stone, ready for home and sleep. Traffic is thin in the early hours, a boon — and a temptation to some of us to run the lights.

— *R. Eleanor Milne*

Teamen: Marcel Joanisse (L), Anton Nielsen (R)

Two hundred and twenty-four blank stones were still to be carved within the Centre Block when I came to the job as Dominion Sculptor in 1962. Thirty of these formed a frieze in the Foyer of the House of Commons, and very soon I was asked to turn this group into a picture history of Canada. In his instructions to me, E.A. Gardner, Chief Architect of Public Works Canada, made only one stipulation: the tale must end before the First World War, because that had already been commemorated in the Memorial Chamber. I was left free to decide how the story would be told and the style of the carving. Four men, all qualified stone carvers, formed the team that would work along with me. Their names were Fernand Rossignol, Roland Rossignol, Iti Busolo, and Wilfrid Filion. When Iti Busolo and Wilfrid Filion retired, Anton Nielsen, Joseph Joanisse, and Maurice Joanisse joined us. As the volume of other work expanded, Marcel Joanisse also became part of the team.

Knowing little of our history in depth, I was eager to learn all I could. My great good luck lay in the generosity of Erik Spicer, the Parliamentary Librarian, who welcomed me to the extensive stacks and gave me unlimited time to work there. Having had no inkling of the riches to be mined, or of their diversity, I was in for a series of wonderful surprises. I found old journals, letters, and diaries, many of them kept by the families of the writers and some willed to the library. Letters sent to those left behind far across the sea in France and England gave me an intimate view into the lives of factors at trading posts, governors' wives, and itinerant physicians. One doctor, whose practice extended from Ottawa to Kingston, recorded an exhausting journey over corduroy

"As an architect, John Pearson [principal architect for the new Centre Block (1916-24),] was pre-eminently an artist, a poet whose material was stone" [*The Ottawa Journal*, June 7, 1940]. Beyond planning and constructing a building for practical purposes, Pearson wanted to record the history of Canada in imperishable forms through stone and woodwork. The architects envisaged on all sides — arches, pillars, walls, gables above doors and windows — carved ornaments symbolizing incidents in Canadian History, such as its institutions, life, industry and nature. The entire building would be alive and vibrant, affording days of pleasant occupation to visitors.

— Audrey Dubé, *Stone Carving in the Parliament Building*

roads, his bones rattling like dice in a cup. The wife of a factor, travelling to her wilderness home in what must have been an enormous canoe, had insisted on bringing her piano as part of the cargo, and a cast iron stove was added to keep the passengers warm. To my delight, I found photographs of paintings made on birch bark, and of watercolours painted by some of the women depicting woodland scenes. Engineers and surveyors, too, had sent back maps and sketches of the territory to their employers in Europe. The library stacks also held autobiographies, works on political matters requested by Senators and Members of Parliament, and, to my intense interest, translations of scientific reports made by Norwegian scientists during their explorations in the Canadian Arctic.

All these marvellous records introduced me to the heart and spirit of those who were so actively involved in the early days of European expansion. They offered me more. They

15

made clear how much the Europeans were indebted to the aboriginal people, often for their very survival. The wisdom, knowledge, and technical skills of the ancient inhabitants and the very different kinds of knowledge and expertise that were brought by the newcomers were soon combined, to the advantage of both. The aboriginal people themselves were also represented in these records, many by taped oral accounts and by papers published by anthropologists. These gave me some insight into the unique cultures and languages, as well as the artistic and engineering genius, of the indigenous peoples who had farmed, fished, hunted, and governed for eons before people from Europe arrived. So the history to be told is a saga of many peoples with many roots.

After months of reading, note-taking, sifting, and refining, I was ready to explore ideas for a design. I wanted to carve a theme in poetic form, that form based on reality. I realized that my vision of Canada, unlike the public art I saw in the government buildings of Washington and London, must be simple, direct, and unsophisticated. And our history must not be confined to human activity: our nation has been shaped by its setting — the flowers, vines, and trees that clothe our land, the fish in our lakes and seas, the birds, the wildlife in our forests, the animals on our ranches and farms, the tundra, the mountains.

In seeking a style that would adapt well to my goals and yet harmonize with the Gothic Revival setting, I drew upon my European experience. Having seen for myself the sculptures in some of the great medieval cathedrals, churches, and abbeys of England, France, and Italy, and having observed their placement and absorbed their contrasts and harmonies, I could recall vividly those elements that could be used to express my own ideas about Canadian history.

I chose the Romanesque style. The architectural frame within which I was to work provided a space for the carving comparable to those in Romanesque structures, and the vivid presentation and flowing movement of its sculptural style, its spontaneity and boldness, supported my ideas. I decided to combine it with the naturalism of a Gothic carving technique whose deep cuts make it possible to create almost free-standing forms — a technique not used before in the Centre Block. The resulting strong contrasts of light and shadow that change as the viewer moves about would give the work a vitality not otherwise attainable. The subtle distortion normal in monumental sculpture would make the forms appear in proper proportion when seen from the floor below. To present the stories in the most compelling way, I would stress simplicity of line and form.

This combination of elements in the design and carving of the frieze would fit naturally into my own approach to sculpture, wherein I explore the inner quality of the material itself — in this case, stone — to express with intensity the dynamism, power, movement, and intrinsic nature of the subject. My artistic style is influenced, no doubt, by my knowledge of the effectiveness of Egyptian and Assyrian monumental sculpture as well as by later European art, but it is now the result of my own artistic growth.

Where to begin? Begin at the beginning, I told myself. Over great spans of time, waves of people arrived on this continent, where they developed new languages and cultures, and established bands, totems, and confederacies. I decided that the first episode in the tale would celebrate the arrival of the first human beings on the northern part of this vast continent, and the last would use two nearly contemporary events to illustrate loyalty to a principle: the destruction of the Acadian colony and its subsequent dispersal as a consequence of its refusal to swear allegiance to the English crown would represent an unbending spirit, while the decision of the United Empire Loyalists to emigrate rather than accept citizenship in a revolutionary republic would display the courage of people willing to take a risk. Both cases would portray loyalty to ancestral ties.

Instead of following the sequence of time, I envisioned a pictorial poem with no real beginning and no end, something like an Edda, where the actions are real but are not necessarily presented in the order in which they took place. Although the stories would be related to one another, the loose weave of their linkages would allow great freedom in presentation.

I developed the theme on three levels, the historical, the sociological, and the philosophical; that is, I began with the facts, depicted what happened in response to these facts, and commented on their meaning, sometimes in allegorical language — as in the stones devoted to peace, education, and freedom. The language of symbol used throughout invites all who come to the Parliament Buildings to read and to understand. My intention was to carve for the lettered and the unlettered, the young and the old.

Because the Speaker of the House has the power to accept or reject any changes made within the House of Commons precinct, I submitted my design proposal to him. The work was accepted. It took a total of about eight years of work to carve the frieze, but we were interrupted by other jobs, so in the end we spent a good part of twelve years of our lives on the project.

As a design office, I had been allotted a small space in the telephone terminal room — Room 113 — where all equipment was exposed and vulnerable. I was told not to touch *anything*. It was an incongruous setting for my drawing board and large sheets of paper.

The carvers' shop, on the other hand, was a lofty basement room situated directly beneath the Senate Foyer. It was amusingly described in the *Montreal Star* of June 2, 1962: "In her workshop in the basement of the parliament buildings, Miss Milne is surrounded by the tools of her trade. Guarding either side of the door into the workshop are a giant lion and unicorn, which are the plaster casts of the stone animals guarding the front entrance of the centre block. Inside the room hundreds of discarded plaster casts line the walls and in one corner Sir John A. Macdonald stands proudly in front of a smiling cherub who seems quite unconcerned about its lack of clothes. In the actual workshop a maze of ladders, wooden horses, discarded drawings and a big clay vat add up to an overall air of confusion."

The members of my team were all trained stone carvers. Several of them discovered particular abilities or specialized skills in the course of working on this project. Iti Busolo had much experience in his craft. He could replicate every detail in conservation reproduction so accurately that it was next to impossible to tell his work from the original. In his youth he had been employed by the great Italian sculptor Marino Marini. Fernand Rossignol, whose father had been on the stone carving staff before him, developed a gift for seeing and sculpting patterns in flowing water and freezing arctic air. Roland Rossignol, his younger brother, fashioned the leaves of water lilies and other plants and brought them to delicate life. Wilfrid Filion, a master of precise detail, gave us clear renderings of fish, grasses, and leaves. Everything that Anton Nielsen, the Danish carver, produced was richly patterned. The first job to which he applied his bold carving style and

Trading in furs and tools　　　　　　RCMP　　　　　　*Voyageurs*

endless patience was the Viking ship. It was he who was entrusted with the carving of the Red River Settlement panel, at a time when I was incapacitated by a serious accident. Joseph Joanisse was a reliable craftsman, limned his work clearly, and, as foreman, organized the work of the group effectively. Maurice Joanisse joined us late in the project. Because of his many talents it was he who won the competition for my job when I retired.

We worked as one — one head with many limbs. It was successful, and it was great.

When we first began working on the frieze, I prepared full-scale models in clay for two of the panels, from which I made plaster moulds. We took these enormous moulds up onto the mezzanine and lowered them onto the scaffold. I carved the human figures and many of the animals while the other carvers cut faithful copies of the supporting detail into the blank stone, using a measuring tool. This was the process to which the team was accustomed when I arrived. However, within the first year the carvers had learned to reproduce my designs without mechanical aids, and so, beginning with the third panel, which is about Native people greeting Vikings, I no longer made clay models and moulds, but drew directly onto the stone in full scale with a charcoal stick. Using small drawings laid out on the floor of the scaffolding as my guide, I could accurately transfer the designs by eye onto the blank stone in the correct scale without using a grid. From that outline, the men roughed in the general form, using power tools. Each of us then took part in the carving. Often, we would work on three panels at one time — one cutting out leaves, another water, I, the figures. Because each carver had the freedom to express his own spirit in the context of the whole, the forms created were full of vitality and depth.

Finding the gold　　　　　*Henry Hudson*　　　　　*Gold!*

Because we carved in place, on stones embedded in the building's structure, we worked at night. The noise and dust we made could not have been borne by the Members of Parliament and the Senators when the Houses were in session, nor by anyone in the building's offices. We were often a full six hours on the job, and had to concentrate intensely all that time. Mistakes were difficult to correct, mainly because we were cutting into the actual fabric of the building. If we cut too deeply or chipped off stone accidentally, we could be faced with a major problem that could force a change in design. And we couldn't send out for new stone. We had other problems as well. Standing on scaffolding, we could not step back to judge our carving as it progressed. Cutting into stone under artificial light, we had to anticipate how the forms would appear in the natural light of day.

Now, as I stand in the centre of the Foyer looking up to the coffered ceiling and the carved fabric that skirts this historic space, I am aware of the many hands that worked the stone, capturing the stories of the peoples of Canada. And I delight in remembering the interest of the parliamentarians (Mr. Trudeau joined us on the scaffold one night) and appreciate their not interfering — not by so much as a suggestion for revision or embellishment.

The *History of Canada Series* complements the Gothic and beaux-arts elements contributed by architects John A. Pearson and Jean Omer Marchand in their designs of 1916. It is in harmony with the carvings done through the years by teams led by Walter Allen and William Oosterhoff, and with those done in the eighties and nineties by individual Aboriginal sculptors. The work is pleasing to me, and, it seems, to others.

THE HISTORY OF CANADA SERIES

PHOTOGRAPHS BY EWALD RICHTER

LEFT PANEL
An Inuit man teaches a boy to hunt

> *I speak with the mouth of Qeqertuanaq and say:*
> *I will walk with leg muscles strong*
> *As the sinews on the shin of a little caribou calf.*
> *I will walk with leg muscles strong*
> *As the sinews on the shin of a little hare.*
> *I will take care not to walk toward the dark.*
> *I will walk toward the day.*

This Igloolik song is one of the magic songs that Aua obtained from Qeqertuanaq, an old woman whose family had handed them down from "the very first people on earth."

CENTRE STONE
The Bluefish Cave people enter life in a new land

In the Bluefish Caves of northern Yukon, archaeologists have found evidence of the use of stone tools between 25,000 and 12,000 years ago.

RIGHT PANEL
The ceremonial hunt

The formal pose of the hunters indicates that they honour the creatures who offer up their lives to them.

*Until recently, the route by which the first migrants came to the Americas was assumed to be the land-bridge that once joined Alaska to the easternmost parts of Asia. However, scientists now believe that ancient travellers arrived in both North and South America by a number of sea routes as well.

LEFT PANEL
An Inuit man teaches a boy to hunt

CENTRE STONE
The Bluefish Cave people enter life in a new land

CENTRE STONE
The Bluefish Cave people enter life in a new land

RIGHT PANEL
The ceremonial hunt

LEFT PANEL
Native people greet Vikings arriving in Newfoundland between 900 and 1000 CE

CENTRE STONE
John Cabot, holding a scroll in his left hand and a tiller in his right.

Under the flag of Henry VII of England, the Italian John Cabot (born Giovanni Caboto) financed his own expedition to the fisheries along the coast of Newfoundland, thus ending the monopoly of fishermen who had kept its location secret.

RIGHT PANEL
Europeans fish off the Grand Banks of Newfoundland

The ship is a caravel, akin to John Cabot's ship, the *Matthew*. The codfish signify the riches in marine life found on the Banks by Cabot and his crew. The abstract trees indicate that the Grand Banks fishing grounds are to be found not far off shore. The large plant forms are stylized kelp.

LEFT PANEL
Native people greet Vikings arriving in Newfoundland between 900 and 1000 CE

CENTRE STONE
John Cabot, holding a scroll in his left hand and a tiller in his right.

CENTRE STONE
John Cabot, holding a scroll in his left hand and a tiller in his right.

RIGHT PANEL
Europeans fish off the Grand Banks of Newfoundland

LEFT PANEL
Jacques Cartier maps the shores of the St. Lawrence River

Cartier stands with his right foot on the shore of the river and his left foot on board his ship. This signifies that he explored the shores of the St. Lawrence River but did not travel inland. In his hands are a scroll and calipers used for mapping. The many moons tell of the passage of time as reckoned by the aboriginal people of this world, a world new to Europeans, who gauged time in a different manner. The large curled plant forms are stylized ferns, indicating that the explorers are in wet land. Members of the expedition find fish, bird and animal life, evergreen trees, and maples.

CENTRE STONE
The first merchant ships navigate the St. Lawrence River

One boat carved above the other represents successive sailings over many years.

RIGHT PANEL
Samuel de Champlain encounters an aboriginal guide willing to lead him inland

Champlain's hand rests on the guide's shoulder, emphasizing his particular rapport with the Native people. The leafless trees imply that he remained in this new territory for more than one full year. The clover forms tell of his success in many of his endeavours, and the plants bearing fruit suggest that the climate was fairly temperate. The water lilies are a sign of the many small rivers and streams along his route. The water flowing in the background indicates that he found a large inland sea.

*Jacques Cartier explored and charted the Gulf of St. Lawrence and the St. Lawrence River in the 1530s and 1540s. Samuel de Champlain, who first arrived in North America in 1603, explored and mapped areas farther inland, clarifying the relationships of the St. Lawrence, Richelieu, and Great Lakes waterways. The work of these great explorers made it possible for later entrepreneurs to move with confidence into the interior of the continent.

LEFT PANEL
Jacques Cartier maps the shores of the St. Lawrence River

CENTRE STONE
The first merchant ships navigate the St. Lawrence River

CENTRE STONE
The first merchant ships navigate the St. Lawrence River

RIGHT PANEL
*Samuel de Champlain encounters an aboriginal guide willing
to lead him inland*

LEFT PANEL
The Battle of the Plains of Abraham, 1759

Clutching at shrubbery, British soldiers are climbing up the cliffs to the fort. The serried lines carved below the battlements describe the field they must cross. Fleurs-de-lys inscribed on the wall identify the fort as belonging to France.

CENTRE STONE
An allegory of life enduring in the midst of strife

A strong tree supports nesting birds while a deer is resting in its shade. This signifies that life goes on in spite of conflict and treaties.

RIGHT PANEL
The Treaty of Paris, 1763

By this treaty, France retained the islands of St. Pierre and Miquelon, but surrendered to England all other territories and claims in North America east of the Mississippi River except New Orleans, and guaranteed unrestrained navigation of certain rivers to all British subjects.

Louis XV of France is passing the scroll of secession to George III of England, as part of the booty from the Seven Years War. The two kings, so casually seated, seem unaware of the true value of these lands.

LEFT PANEL
The Battle of the Plains of Abraham, 1759

CENTRE STONE
An allegory of life enduring in the midst of strife

CENTRE STONE
An allegory of life enduring in the midst of strife

RIGHT PANEL
The Treaty of Paris, 1763

LEFT PANEL
The first colony, 1763

England grants colonial status to Quebec under the name "Lower Canada." The arms of Quebec standing between George III and a kneeling figure represent the royal grant.

CENTRE STONE
A family of European settlers establishes a homestead

Because boundaries are now set, young families begin to build homes in the wilderness. A young man and woman stand together, her hand on his. She points out the site of their homestead. Their small child, holding his pet, is secure. This family speaks for the many who began farming in this new land.

RIGHT PANEL
The Battle of Queenston Heights, 1812

The Battle of Queenston Heights contributed to the establishment of an agreed border between Canada and the United States.

General Brock, mounted on his horse, is leading his soldiers in battle against the invading Americans. The small fleeing figure in the lower right signifies the defeat of the American forces, who are retreating into the waves of the Niagara River. The leaping tongues of fire in the upper right indicate the ferocity of the fight.

LEFT PANEL
The first colony, 1763

CENTRE STONE
A family of European settlers establishes a homestead

CENTRE STONE
A family of European settlers establishes a homestead

RIGHT PANEL
The Battle of Queenston Heights, 1812

LEFT PANEL
Christians and Native people meet

The figure wearing a cassock represents the religious orders that arrived in the early seventeenth century. The plain cross signifies that other Christians also spoke of their faith with the native people. Through their marvellously detailed journals, the Jesuits informed their Society in France about aboriginal spirituality.

CENTRE STONE
An allegory of education

An allegorical figure offers fruit from the Tree of Knowledge. An infant, protected by the large tree, is looking at an open book while a larger child is reaching on his own for the fruit high up among strong branches.

RIGHT PANEL
A woman teaches a group of children

Seated outdoors, a woman is teaching little children from a book. The pastoral setting indicates that formal schooling was not yet established.

LEFT PANEL
Christians and Native people meet

CENTRE STONE
An allegory of education

CENTRE STONE
An allegory of education

RIGHT PANEL
A woman teaches a group of children

LEFT PANEL
The Red River settlement

A man, sleeves rolled to the elbow, clears a place in the wilderness. A woman broadcasts seed into the newly cleared soil. The Red River flows across the open land. The cart is standing ready to carry the harvest home. This panel covers a time-cycle from first clearing to harvest.

CENTRE STONE
David Thompson, surveyor and map-maker

David Thompson, or 'Koo-Koo-Sint' [Star-Looker], a superb surveyor and map-maker, explored western North America between 1784 and 1812, found the source of the Columbia River and charted its entire length. His work in the midwest was invaluable to the engineers who designed the route for the railroad.

RIGHT PANEL
The railroad links east to west

A powerful figure is thrusting mountains apart. The Pacific dogwood, representing the Province of British Columbia, identifies the geographical setting. The detail of a train entering a tunnel represents the feat of drilling into living rock to allow passage of the rails.

*Until Canada was united by rail from sea to sea the country could not function as a whole community, and it was the settlement of the Red River Valley that made the railroad link between east and west possible.

LEFT PANEL
The Red River settlement

CENTRE STONE
David Thompson, surveyor and map-maker

CENTRE STONE
David Thompson, surveyor and map-maker

RIGHT PANEL
The railroad links east to west

LEFT PANEL
The fur trade

Within a forest of beech, maple, and birch, an aboriginal chief, accompanied by one of his tribe, is negotiating with a merchant fur trader, who also has an assistant. The trader is bartering an axe for a pelt. The axe handle is resting against his knee; the large pelt lies across the lap of the Indian.

CENTRE STONE
Banking is founded in Canada

With the establishment of Canada's banking system, the country became financially independent of England.
A banker holds scrolls, representing mortgages and loans.

RIGHT PANEL
Les Voyageurs

The whole trading system depended on the strength of those who brought out freight from the back country.
Four voyageurs in the forward part of the canoe paddle down swiftly running waters on a day of hot sun. The shrubby growth behind them and the low range of mountains in the background indicate that they are travelling through fairly level country.

LEFT PANEL
The fur trade

CENTRE STONE
Banking is founded in Canada

CENTRE STONE
Banking is founded in Canada

RIGHT PANEL
Les Voyageurs

LEFT PANEL
The position of the North Magnetic Pole is determined

A figure dressed in parka and mukluks leans into strong winds as he anchors a marker flag at the North Magnetic Pole. Stars and jagged lines tell of the darkness and cold of the High Arctic.

CENTRE STONE
An officer of the North West Mounted Police dressed for the Arctic

The lone figure with his team of dogs represents the North West Mounted Police, who were the first to keep order in this remote region of Canada. Established in 1873, this law-enforcement body continues as the Royal Canadian Mounted Police.

RIGHT PANEL
Panning for gold in the Yukon Territory

The kneeling figure dipping his pan into fast-running water tells of the hardship endured by those who joined the rush for gold. The tent is a fragile shelter against frost and heat, and the mountain lion reminds us that life was not always secure in this wild place. The mules, seen drinking from the river, were the panner's only form of transport.

There's gold and it's haunting and haunting;
*   It's luring me on as of old;*
Yet it isn't the gold that I'm wanting
*   So much as just finding the gold.*
It's the great, big, broad land way up yonder,
*   It's the forests where silence has lease:*
It's the beauty that thrills me with wonder,
*   It's the stillness that fills me with peace.*
*   — Robert W. Service, "The Spell of the Yukon"*

LEFT PANEL
The position of the North Magnetic Pole is determined

CENTRE STONE
An officer of the North West Mounted Police dressed for the Arctic

CENTRE STONE
An officer of the North West Mounted Police dressed for the Arctic

RIGHT PANEL
Panning for gold in the Yukon Territory

LEFT PANEL
The destruction of the Acadian colony, 1755

The Acadians, a community of settlers of French origin established since 1605 in what is now the Maritime provinces, accepted English sovereignty but refused to swear allegiance to the English Crown. In response, the conquerors carried out a mass deportation.

Women and children are forcibly separated from their husbands and fathers by determined soldiers. The mother, pushed away by the soldiers, hasn't had time to dress her naked child. The dog is excited, knowing that something dreadful is happening. Flames leaping from the church mark the burning of the village.

CENTRE STONE
An allegory of freedom

A strong figure is breaking chains, freeing doves. This speaks a symbolic language stating that those who come to this land to begin anew must leave all rage and bias behind.

RIGHT PANEL
The arrival of the United Empire Loyalists

A man, a woman, and two children, representing the many families who came to Canada after the American Revolution, are greeted by those already established on the land. The thick growth of leaves tells of the difficulties they encountered on their way.

LEFT PANEL
The destruction of the Acadian colony, 1755

CENTRE STONE
An allegory of freedom

CENTRE STONE
An allegory of freedom

RIGHT PANEL
The arrival of the United Empire Loyalists

The series is carved in Indiana limestone, a medium-soft stone entirely without grain made up of billions of sea creatures called ooilites, which lived in ancient seas in many parts of the world. After they died and fell to the sea floor, the great weight of water compacted them over millions of years and turned them into a very beautiful stone. The absence of grain means that the carver's tool can cut in any direction with minimum risk of breaking the stone. This allows great freedom when cutting details such as leaves, branches, and other small forms. Some parts are detached from the main sculpted surface deeply enough to permit the carver to put a hand behind them. The resulting rich, dark shadows give a rhythmic flow to the sculpture as a whole.

The finished work is carved in stone 18 centimetres (7 $1/4$ inches) thick to an average depth of 7.5 centimetres (3 inches) and a maximum depth of 13 centimetres (5 $1/8$ inches).

Many times I have been asked about the strength needed for sculpture. Although most of my work is done with a chisel and mallet, there isn't a great deal of strength involved. The trick is in the balance.

The tools employed when carving the *History of Canada Series* are basically the same in style and weight as those employed by sculptors in stone down through the ages: a three pound square-head mallet and point to rough out the form; a two pound and one pound mallet for less heavy roughing out of the stone; and a one pound, one-half pound, and one-quarter pound mallet for all finishing work.

Hand sculpture tools are made of forged steel. The cutting blades of pneumatic power tools are made of carbide steel and set into a forged steel shank. These carving tools are an extension of one's body and hands, arms and fingers. Hand tools are sharpened with a washita or equivalent stone; power tools with green stone carborundum wheels.

To use a hand-tool successfully and easily one must lean into the work. The whole body is involved in the action — the arms and hands direct the carving of form, while the body supplies weight and pressure to the knife blade of the tool.

When carving with a power-tool one must apply the weight of the body against the tool much more delicately. The pneumatic hammer, which adds power to the stroke, must be carefully curbed and controlled.

Depth of cut, surface finish, detail of whatever sort — all are the product of a continuous dialogue between the whole body, the whole mind and spirit.

The point chisel, tooth chisel, and hand drill are used in the roughing out of forms. The half-pound mallet and the quarter-pound mallet are used for final finishing and refining.

The cutting tools are the point, the channel bit, and the straight chisel; a spoon blade is also very useful. The tooth chisel is designed primarily to handle partially finished surfaces and to give texture, by trapping light on the surface of forms. When carving for the effect of light reflection one must use this technique with caution.

Surrounded by tools and air hose on the scaffold, Eleanor Milne carves "Cabot."

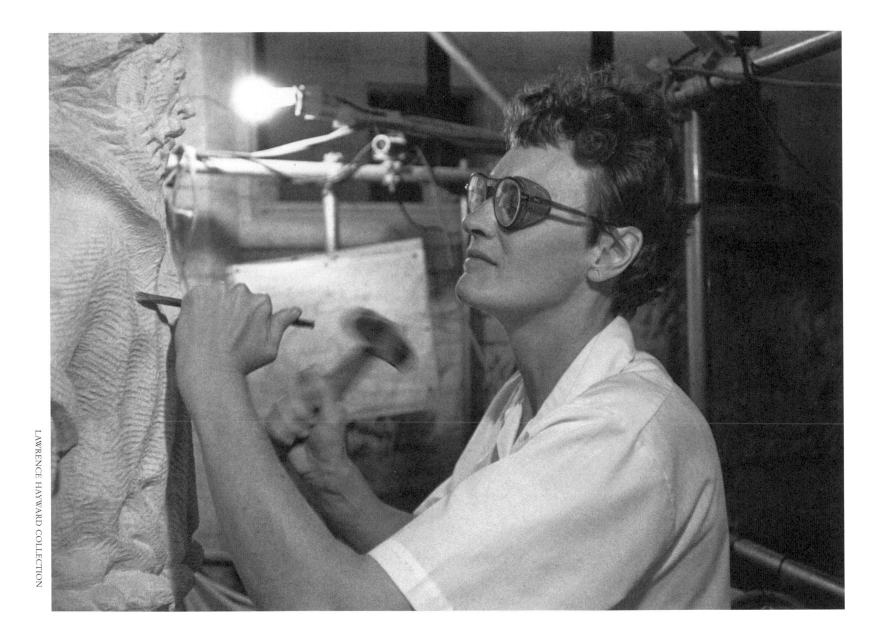

86   *This photograph displays the use of a tooth chisel with a one pound hammer.*

The power tools, which are used with a pneumatic hammer, closely resemble the hand-carving blades and points, with the exception of the bush hammer. This tool is used to make deep shadows where they are required for dramatic effect, and level surfaces in backgrounds. Here Joseph Joanisse uses a heavy drill bit.

Tapping musical notes from the stone masts, Fernand Rossignol made a quiet tone poem of his carving. Here he is using a light drill bit, which requires delicate finger turning.

A sampling of hand tools and hammers.

An array of power-tools and a pneumatic hammer.

x

y

w

b

d

f

h

j

n

p

r

t

bb

dd

ff

hh

jj

ll

nn

ELEANOR MILNE COLLECTION

88

HISTORICAL NOTES

A. Artists and Craftsmen of the Centre Block

• *Resident Designers, Sculptors, and Carvers*

This book describes only one work by one master sculptor and a team of seven carvers, who carried it out between 1962 and 1974. The embellishment of the Centre Block as a whole, however, began in 1916, the same year as its construction began, after fire had completely destroyed its predecessor, sparing only the Parliamentary Library. Carving has continued intermittently until today, interrupted only by the Great Depression and the Second World War.

The principal artists and craftsmen who produced the carvings in the Centre Block are listed here:

J.H. Bonnor, superintendent in charge of modelling and sculpture work, 1916. An Englishman well qualified in Gothic ornamentation, Bonner died soon after his appointment, but his staff of four had already begun modelling, making plaster casts, and carving the capitals, animals, and grotesques for the building exterior.

Walter J. Allen, superintendent of the modelling and carving shop, 1917–1924. Experienced in stone and woodwork in Great Britain and the Continent, he was well known for his work on British cathedrals. Allen designed and, with his team of four to seven men, executed works in stone, wood, and plaster. These included the decorative moulding of the ten arches in the Foyer of the House of Commons, incorporating foliage, fabulous animals, imps, and masks (1919–1920).

Cléophas Soucy. Born in Quebec, Soucy began carving and modelling in clay for the Parliament Buildings in 1919 and retired as Dominion Stone Carver in 1950. His contributions were significant: he completed the exterior as well as much work on the interior. After architect Allen Keefer drew up the designs, Soucy made full-scale clay models from which his staff made copies in stone.

William Oosterhoff, Dominion Stone Carver, 1950–1962. Born in Holland, he had been a member of Soucy's team. He would make an exact clay model of each design and have it cast in plaster; his carving team would then reproduce it down to the finest detail. Among other work, in 1953 he and his team carved a narrow frieze near the ceiling in the House of Commons Foyer, using themes representative of the natural resources of Canada.

Eleanor Milne, Dominion Sculptor, 1962–1993. Born in Saint John, New Brunswick. Over time, her stone carving team included seven men, but the work was not confined to stone and wood carving. Aside from the monumental frieze in the Foyer of the House of Commons and, within its Chamber, the large stone panels — the *British North America Act Series* and the *Evolution of Life Series* — the team did building restoration and maintenance. Milne herself worked in various media, responded to many special requests for design and sculpture, gave artistic advice, and supervised the work of others.

Maurice Joanisse, Chief Sculptor, 1993– . A native of Ottawa, he started working in stone at the age of twelve in his father's cemetery monument business, and acquired further skills upon joining Milne's stone carving team in 1971. Among other work, he carved the *Evolution of Life Series* and part of the British North America Series to Milne's designs.

89

- *Native Sculptors Program*

In 1980, in order to include the artistic expression of the First Nations and Inuit in the Parliament Buildings, aboriginal artists were invited to take part in a juried competition: to design and carve work to be installed over doors in the House of Commons area. Large stone panels of Indiana Limestone or Steatite were shipped to the winners to be sculpted in their own workshops. The artists and their works are listed below.

Walter Harris, a hereditary chief of the village of Kispiox in northwest British Columbia. *Killer Whale* (1981). A traditional killer whale crest is attended by grouse and human figures (Commonwealth Room).

Guy Sioui, Odanak, Quebec. *Head of Arrow* (1982–1983). Steatite. An arrowhead with tobacco leaves symbolizes peace. It is outlined with motifs of Wendat and Iroquois pottery. A double curve, an Algonquin motif, represents the power of plants (Room 223-S).

Pauloosie Akitirk, Arctic Bay, Nunavut (1982). An Inuk holds the tusks of a whale, honouring the mammal for providing food, heating oil, and revenue from the sale of its tusks (Room 219-S).

Abraham Anghik, Salt Spring Island, British Columbia, has also lived in Paulatuk, Inuvik, Yellowknife, and Vancouver. *Life Cycle* (1981) presents many themes: a snowy owl signifies the noble aspect of human nature; an Inuit man represents a shaman; a woman represents the sea goddess, Sedna; four seals symbolize north, south, east, and west, the four seasons, and the food cycle; mask images represent ritual Inuit culture from Siberia to Greenland; two ravens are reminders of legends, and inside these birds are embryos, the potential for life (Room 209-S).

Geeshee Akulukjuk, Pangnirtung, Nunavut. *Inuit Shaman* (1981–1982). A long-haired Inuit shaman in ecstatic trance, performs a ritual dance (Room 207-S).

Kumakuluk Saggiak, Cape Dorset, Nunavut (1990). Saggiak's favourite subjects — birds, whales, seal, bear, snake, and muskox — reflect the hunting life of his people (Room 203-S).

Earl Muldon, Hazelton, British Columbia (1982–1983). A five-panel sculpture depicts West Coast First Nations family crests of the Frog, Owl and Wolf clans, with totem figures at each end (East side, Members' Entrance stairway).

Joseph Jacobs, Curve Lake Reserve, Ontario. *Creation* (1982–1986). A five-panel carving depicts the legend of the creation of the earth and of good and evil, and the formation of the Iroquois Confederacy. In the centre of the five panels is *To-do-da-ho*, a mythic snake-haired wizard who helped found the confederacy (West side, Members' Entrance Stairway).

B. Styles of Architecture and Art

- *Romanesque Architecture and Art*

Architecture: The Romanesque style emerged in Italy around 500 CE, gradually spread across western Europe, and then, about 1200 CE, began to give way to the Gothic style, which evolved when the round arch was discarded in favour of the pointed one. The Romanesque style may be recognized by its massive masonry wall construction and its rounded vaults and arches. Narrow windows in the long supporting walls constricted the amount of natural light, but the sombre interiors were sometimes warmed by colourful frescoes. Notable examples are found in Vézelay and Toulouse in France, and Durham in England.

Art: Carving was an integral part of Romanesque stone masonry: on capitals (the tops of columns), on the receding arches of doorways, and on the half-circle of the tympanum (the space enclosed by the top of the door frame and the upper part of the arch). Decorative, energetic, vital, and filled with the symbols of medieval belief, the carvings greatly enhance both the effect and the meaning of the structures they adorn.

- *Gothic Architecture and Art*

Architecture: The Gothic style emerged in France in the twelfth century, spread throughout Europe, and flourished until the sixteenth century. It may be recognized by the lancet arch (narrow, acutely pointed), the ribbed vault (an arched structure that forms a roof or ceiling, with projecting moulds or bands on the underside that form the framework or structure for the vault), and the flying buttress (an exterior arch that supports a wall by transmitting the thrust outward and downward). For structural reasons, these elements allow a building to rise to great heights, enclose wide spaces, and be flooded with natural light. In an age of intellectual ferment, international flow of ideas, and deep religious feeling, when a whole community, from the highest to the lowest, would join in building a cathedral, the desire to reach upward, to be lifted into the light, was a major impetus behind the popularity of this style. Notable examples are Chartres, Notre Dame de Paris, and Rheims cathedrals in France, and Salisbury Cathedral in England.

Art: The side walls are no longer required to hold up the roof, so huge window openings can be filled with beautifully designed and colourful stained glass. Stone carving is more lifelike than before. Plant forms such as leaves are deeply undercut, and human faces are no longer almost featureless

Byzantine masks but look like real European men and women. On early buildings, carvings are merely a harmonious part of the overall architectural form, but later sculptures are more detached from their structural frame, reflecting the desire for a more realistic representation of people and the natural world.

- *Gothic Revival (also known as Neo-Gothic) Architecture and Art*

The Gothic Revival style was popular between the late eighteenth and the late nineteenth centuries. The Houses of Parliament in London, England, and Canada's Parliament Buildings are examples. When the original Centre Block of the Parliament Buildings had to be replaced after the 1917 fire that left only the Parliamentary Library intact, Gothic Revival was still thought the most appropriate style for the visible demonstration of a nation's pride. However, by 1917 society's desire for architectural fantasy and romance had given way to a less optimistic outlook on life. The style of the present buildings has a formal dignity in keeping with the temper of its time, but it still provides great scope for an authentically Gothic spirit in its ornamentation. The design needs are similar to those of an earlier age — to span wide spaces and rise to great heights, to provide appropriate shelter for specific activities, to express the values of the times — but very different expectations of comfort, convenience and safety require very different construction methods and technical skills. The work of the sculptors who carve the stones is very little changed from medieval times: the tools remain basically the same, and it may still take months, as it did in the past, to complete a single sculpture, and years to fully express the spirit of the building.

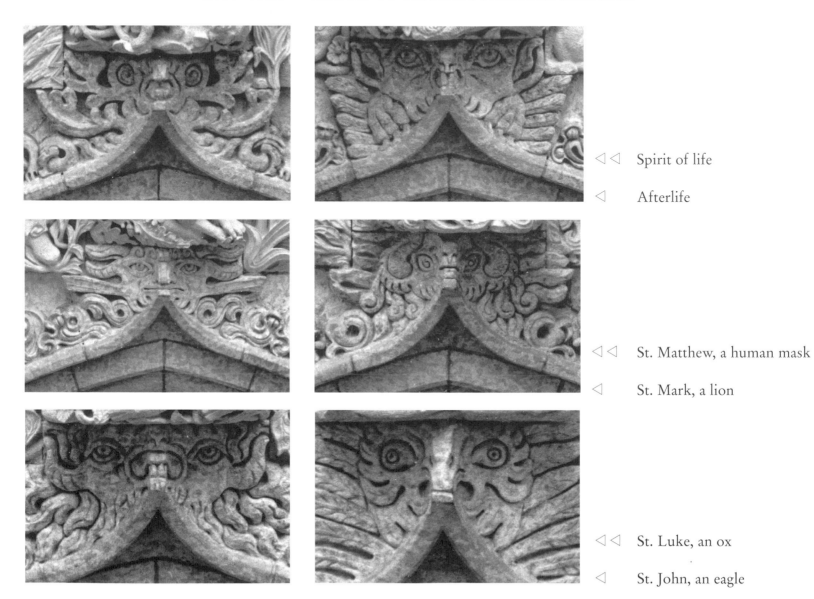

◁ ◁   Spirit of life

◁   Afterlife

◁ ◁   St. Matthew, a human mask

◁   St. Mark, a lion

◁ ◁   St. Luke, an ox

◁   St. John, an eagle

Pipes and stringed instrument ▷ ▷

A harp and a drum ▷

Located beneath the centre stones of the arches, each of the respective ten keystones represents an aspect of Canada's spiritual heritage. Life and Afterlife represent Aboriginal spirituality. Human, lion, ox, and eagle masks represent the Book of Revelation's living creatures. Musical instruments and the human voice represent the six tones of medieval music. Lion and lamb resting together represent peace between nations.

A trumpet and human voice ▷

Peace ▷

RELATED READING

Canada's Parliament. Ottawa: House of Commons, 1987

Dickason, Olive Patricia, *Canada's First Nations:
A History of Founding Peoples from Earliest Times*, 3rd ed.
Toronto: Oxford University Press, 2002.

Dubé, Audrey, *Stone Carving in the Parliament Building*
(Research Paper: Draft). Ottawa: House of Commons, 1989.

Gardner, Helen, *Art Through the Ages*. 3rd. ed.
New York: Harcourt Brace and Company, 1948.

Gowans, Alan, *Looking at Architecture in Canada*. Toronto:
Oxford University Press, 1958.

Heritage Conservation Program, *Conservation Guidelines
for the Interior of the Centre Block, Parliament Hill* (Final
Draft). Ottawa: Public Works RPS (CH/EC), 1998.

Kerr, D.D.G., ed., *A Historical Atlas of Canada*. Toronto:
Thomas Nelson and Sons, 1960.

National Film Board of Canada, *Stones of History: Canada's
Houses of Parliament: A Photographic Essay*. Ottawa:
Queen's Printer, 1967.

For those who are familiar with Penumbra's publications in the visual arts, *Captured In Stone* is a wonderful companion. Unlike the others, however, the present volume features the artwork itself rather than the biographies of the principals. This is an intentional decision so that readers may appreciate the full extent of the *History of Canada Series* and enjoy it without reference to any scholarly or academic apparatus. The full-page spreads of the panels are intended to emulate the experience of viewing details of the artwork from the floor of the foyer at the entrance to the House of Commons in Ottawa's Parliament Buildings.

MARGARET WADE LABARGE is a medieval historian. Educated at Radcliffe College, Harvard University, and St. Anne's College, Oxford, she is a member of the Order of Canada and a fellow of the Royal Society of Canada. The author of nine books on themes related to the medieval period, Margaret Wade Labarge has received honorary degrees from Carleton University and the University of Waterloo, and, in 2001, Carleton University's Founders Award.

EWALD RICHTER is an internationally known professional photographer with over forty years experience in all aspects of creative photography and darkroom techniques. Prior to establishing his own company in 1982, Mr. Richter was Chief Photographer for the National Capital Commission.

R. ELEANOR MILNE, Master Sculptor, was educated at the Montreal Museum School of Fine Arts, l'École des Beaux-Arts, Central College of Arts and Crafts in London, England, and the University of Syracuse. She was Dominion Sculptor, Government of Canada from 1962 until her retirement in 1993. Miss Milne is a member of the Order of Canada and the Royal Canadian Academy of Arts. She has received honorary degrees from Carleton University, the University of Windsor, Queen's University, and York University.

K. BARBARA LAMBERT, B.Arch. (McGill), is a freelance writer specializing in architecture, heritage conservation, town planning, and industrial design. She has been a Commissioner of the National Capital Commission and a member of the National Design Council. Her part in this book was inspired by watching the creation of the *History of Canada Series* from her viewpoint as Eleanor Milne's sister.

ELEANOR MOORE is a practising pharmacist and a graduate student in Canadian Studies at Carleton University. Her interest in the *History of Canada Series* sparked research into various aspects of Canadian history and culture, which in turn proved to be an invaluable resource for her collaborative role in this project.